Baldy

Written by Jack Gabolinscy

Illustrated by Richard Hoit

One night, when Eddie and his family were driving
home through the Blue Mountains in Australia, the car
headlights caught two bright red eyes staring from
the middle of the road. They were the eyes of a big,
black possum. Dad tried to stop, but it was too late.
Thump! The car hit it.

Eddie got out of the car. "I'll get it off the road,"
he said. He picked the dead possum up and carried
it onto the grass. Then he did a strange thing. He
removed a shoe, took his sock off and put something
in it. When he returned to the car, he was holding the
sock in his hands. "It's a baby," he said. "It was in the
mother's pouch. It's still alive."

At home, the family gathered around to look at the baby possum. It was pink and tiny. It lay wriggling in the folds of Eddie's sock.

"Yuk! It's ugly. It's as bald as a grub," said Jack. "And it's got a big head like a baby rat."

"It's not ugly. It's beautiful," said Mum.

"It's too young to save," said Dad. "It needs its mother's milk."

"I'll feed it with an eye-dropper," said Eddie. "I'll keep it in my sock in the hot water cupboard."

"It's too young," said Dad. "Its eyes aren't even open."

"I'm going to try," said Eddie. "You never know."

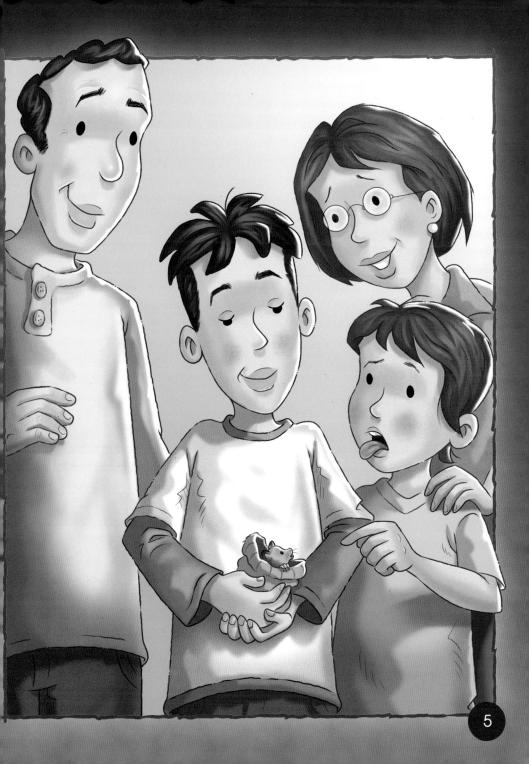

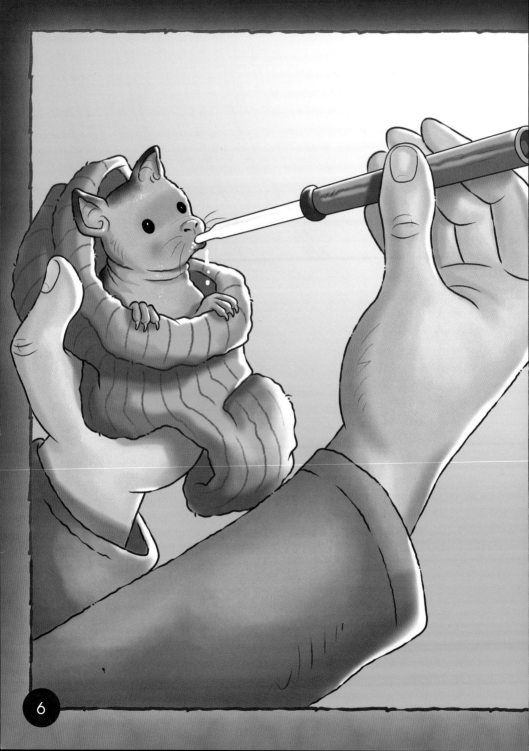

Eddie fitted a tiny rubber tube to the end of an eye-dropper, filled it with milk and held it to the little possum's mouth. It sucked on the soft rubber and drank. Eddie folded it into his sock and put it in a small box on the floor of the hot water cupboard.

"It might be dead by morning," Dad warned again. "A baby as young as that can't live without its mother."

"Yeah!" Jack agreed. "Baldy will be dead in the morning."

"I like that name," said Eddie, ignoring his unkind words. "Baldy. We'll call him Baldy."

Baldy wasn't dead next morning. He was hungry. In the night, he had sucked his eye-dropper dry. Eddie filled it again and Baldy clamped his mouth back on it. Every few hours, Eddie refilled the dropper. Baldy sucked, wriggled, stretched and slept some more.

Baldy grew bigger every day. His eyes opened. His fur grew. Eddie made him a bigger feeder from a medicine bottle. Baldy cuddled into his hands and crawled across his lap.

"Mother Eddie," laughed Mum. "He thinks you are his mother."

"Good," said Eddie. "A baby needs a mother."

Baldy outgrew the hot water cupboard and shifted into a cardboard carton on the kitchen floor. He didn't like the daylight so he slept during the day and woke up at night. In the middle of the night, they often heard his claws scratching across the hard floor on his way to Eddie's bed.

Baldy loved to play. The boys tossed shiny buttons around the sitting room floor. One at a time, he searched them out and stored them in his bed. They hid pieces of apple and carrot in their pockets and shoes, but his clever nose quickly found them.

They played hide-and-seek around the trees with him. He climbed the trees and chuckled his cheeky, chattery call down at them. He was a wonderful pet.

The boys loved Baldy, but as he grew older he grew harder to live with. He left long scratch marks in the wallpaper. He tore the curtains. He knocked vases and lamps off the shelves. He left piles of poo and puddles of pee on the floors and chairs.

One day, Mum made a cake for Dad's birthday. She iced it and put it on the table. Unfortunately, Baldy found it, knocked it off the table, ate some and trampled the rest all over the kitchen.

Mum was as angry as a thunderstorm. "He's got to go," she shouted. "**He's wrecking the house. He's driving me crazy.**"

The next day, Dad was in the orchard. He noticed that all the apples had big bites in them. He looked at the peaches. They were the same. The plums, pears and oranges were the same, too. All the fruit was ruined.

"Possums," grumbled Dad. "They've bitten every piece of fruit in the orchard."

Just then, a cheeky chuckle came from the sleeping box Eddie had made for Baldy in a plum tree. **"Ch-ch-ch-ch-ch-ch!"**

Dad suddenly realised that it wasn't possums that had ruined his fruit. It was one possum. Baldy! His face went red. **"That possum has got to go,"** he roared.

That night, there was a family meeting. "Baldy has to go," said Mum.

"Yes," agreed Dad. "It's time for him to go back to his own world."

"I'll build an outside cage for him," said Eddie hopefully.

"No," said Mum. "If you love him, you'll set him free."

Jack didn't say anything. He felt sorry for Eddie. Long after the rest of the family left the table, Eddie sat there, his chin in his hands, tears trickling down his cheeks. After a while, he got up. "I'll be back soon," he said.

"Don't go far," warned Mum.

"Turn the outside light on," said Dad.
"It'll help you find your way back."

Eddie looked really sad, but he took Baldy and
disappeared out the door. A long time later,
Jack heard him come home. He went straight to
his bedroom.

The family all missed Baldy. They even missed standing or sitting in the wet, dirty patches he left on the floors and chairs. Eddie missed him more than any of them, though. Sometimes, after dinner, he'd stand in the shadows of the orchard, listening and looking into the dark bushes. But they never saw Baldy again. He was back in the Blue Mountains where he came from.

Baldy is a **Narrative**.

A **narrative** has an introduction. It tells . . .

- **who** the story is about (the characters)
- **where** the story happened
- **when** the story happened.

Introduction	
Who	
Where	
When	One night, when Eddie and his family were driving home

A narrative has a **problem** and a **solution**.

Problem

Solution

▬▬▬ Guide Notes

Title: Baldy
Stage: Fluency

Text Form: Narrative
Approach: Guided Reading
Processes: Thinking Critically, Exploring Language, Processing Information
Written and Visual Focus: Illustrative Text

THINKING CRITICALLY
(sample questions)
- What do you think this story could be about? Look at the title and discuss.
- Look at the cover. What kind of animal is on the boy's shoulder? Why do you think the boy might be feeding him?
- Look at pages 2 and 3. Do you think Eddie should have rescued the baby possum? Why or why not?
- Look at pages 8 and 9. Do you think a baby possum would be a good pet? Why or why not?
- Look at pages 10 and 11. What do you think the family should do about Baldy? Why do you think that?
- Look at pages 14 and 15. What does, "If you love him, you'll set him free" mean? Do you agree?
- Look at pages 16 and 17. Do you think it was better for Baldy to be in the wild? Why do you think that?

EXPLORING LANGUAGE

Terminology
Spread, author and illustrator credits, imprint information, ISBN number

Vocabulary
Clarify: Blue Mountains in Australia, possum, pouch, claws, orchard
Adjectives: *soft* rubber, *shiny* buttons, *clever* nose
Pronouns: they, it, he, its, his, you, him, them
Simile: as angry *as a thunderstorm*
Focus the students' attention on **homonyms**, **antonyms** and **synonyms** if appropriate.